Stupid
Poems
5

GW00703307

Ian Vannoey

Stupid Poems

5

Matador
5 Weir Road
Kibworth
Leicester LE8 0LQ, UK
Tel: (+44) 116 2792299
Email: books@troubador.co.uk
Web: www.troubador.co.uk/matador

British Library Cataloguing in Publication Data.
A catalogue record for this book is available from the British Library.

ISBN 9781848763234

Typeset in 11pt Times New Roman by Troubador Publishing Ltd, Leicester, UK

Matador is an imprint of Troubador Publishing Ltd

Contents

Porgy and Bess

We're with the folk of Catfish Row, in South Carolina.
Summertime, the livin's easy, the weather can't be finer.
The women prepare vegetables, the guys are playing dice.
Crown is big and strong but is really not too nice.
His woman is called Bess, and, like him, likes a tipple.
Our hero Porgy's soft on her but, sadly, is a cripple.
Sportin' Life is flash, but is a little rat.
He peddles dope ('happy dust'), and keeps it in his hat.
Then Crown murders Robbins, when over dice they fight.
Now he is a murderer, and runs off in the night.
Porgy takes in Bess; they live blissfully together.
He's got plenty o' nuttin', and is a happy feller.
Serena holds a wake for Robbins, as his death is recent.
She has trouble raising money for a burial that's decent.
They all go for a picnic, held on Kittiwah Isle.
It will be a lot of fun; they really need a smile.
Porgy cannot go, but says that Bess must go too:
'Bess, you is my woman now, you must sing and dance for two.'
Sportin' Life gives a religiously sceptical show:
'The things that you're li'ble to read in the Bible, it ain't necessarily so'.
Now it's time to go, so to the boat they rush.
Crown, who's been hiding there, springs up from out a bush.
He grabs hold of Bess, and showers her with kisses.
He stops her from leaving, so the boat she misses.
When she finally comes home, she is ill with fever.

They pray to Jesus for her life, and luckily they save her.
They shelter from a hurricane; the weather now is squalid.
Crown turns up for Bess, and to Porgy he is horrid.
The hurricane makes a really loud and truly awesome sound:
'De Lawd shake de heavens and de Lawd rock de groun'.'
Jake has gone fishing on de Blackfish Banks, no matter what de wedder say,
He had not guessed it was going to be such a windy day.
Clara is so scared for him; it turns out she is right,
For his boat comes back empty and upside-down that night.
Unfortunately he's drowned, so there is another funeral.
Porgy kills Crown, as was bound to happen sooner or
Later. Everybody thinks that Porgy's done no wrong,
For Crown was a bully, and had it coming all along.
Porgy has to go off to the police station.
When he comes back, he finds the situation
Is that Bess is now with Sportin' Life; they've gone off to New York.
He is devastated, and doesn't give a thought.
Even though he's so disabled, he can hardly stand,
He chases after Bess; he's on his way to a heavenly land.

Greeting Messages for the Equinox

To celebrate the equinox,
I'm sending you a box of chocs.

We will have a lot of fun.
The Equator's underneath the sun.

At these special times of year,
Let's all drink a lot of beer.
The equinoxes come, remember,
One in March; one September.

In Ecuador and Cameroon
The sun is overhead at noon.
There is no time that is greater.
The sun is crossing the Equator.

We can be bright and gay.
There's equal night and day.
We can be gay and bright.
There's equal day and night.

It makes for the seasons, and it is terrific.
The equatorial plane's inclined to the Ecliptic.

Happy equinox.
Don't get chicken pox.

A group of twentieth century physicists argue over the purchase of a new gadget

Said Albert Einstein:
'This is real fine'.
Richard Feynman
Said: 'Real fine, man!'
'A humdinger!'
Said Schrödinger.
'Now you're talking',
Said Stephen Hawking.
But Ernest Rutherford
Used another word.
Wolfgang Pauli
Said 'What folly!'
Marie Curie
Showed her fury.
Max Born
Just showed scorn.
Niels Bohr
Asked what it's for.
'It won't work'
Said Heisenberg.

Enrico Fermi:
'It makes me squirm.' He
Said 'A waste.
It's got no taste'.
Max Planck
Just looked blank.
So Paul Dirac
Took it back.

Salome

From a play by Oscar Wilde, Richard Strauss wrote an opera,
Which caused a scandal in its day, and still it is a shocker.
Herod is the king, and ruler of Judaea.
He's married to Herodias; Salome's his step-daughter.
John the Baptist is a prisoner; he is good at prophecy.
Salome gets to see him, and he takes her fancy.
She says: 'Let me kiss your mouth, I really am not fussy',
But John the Baptist says to her: 'Away you little hussy'.
Herod his step-daughter Salome he fancies.
So the dance of the seven veils, for him alone, she dances.
Herod has promised her that after her striptease,
She could then ask of him anything she please.
The thing that she wants is really rather odd.
It's not a DVD player, or a brand new i-pod.
It's not a world cruise, or a new car for that matter.
She wants the head of John the Baptist on a silver platter.
So she finally gets her wish; the Baptist's mouth she's kissing.
She doesn't seem to mind that most of him is missing.
This is quite perverted; it's gruesome and it's gory.
Herod has her killed; that's the end of the story.

Curry Snobbery

Beef madras
Is upper class.
Rogan josh
Is quite posh.
Vindaloo
Is classy too.
Nan bread
Is well bred.
The jet-set
Often get
Birianis
At their parties.
If you wish
To be quite swish,
Pilau rice
Is very nice.
So while your butler
Brings a korma
Or massala
To your parlour,
Hoi polloi
Get their joy
In a caff
From food that's naff.

Hiawatha on an oil rig (apologies to Longfellow)

By the shores of stormy North Sea,
By the shining big sea water,
Stood a mighty oil riggy,
Owned by Shell or owned by BP.
To the mighty oil riggy
Came a man from Aberdeen
In a great big helicopter.
When the great big helicopter
Landed on the oil riggy,
Then the man from Aberdeen
Got down from the helicopter,
Stood upon the oil riggy.
He was dying for a ciggy,
He was gasping for a smoky,
So he took and lit a ciggy,
But the foreman bloody angry:
'Do you take me for a loony?
On the rig there is no smoky'.
So the man from Aberdeen
Got back on the helicopter,
Flew back in the helicopter.
No smoking in the helicopter.
When he got to Aberdeen,
There he had a great big smoky.

People called Alistair

Alistair Sim used to be funny.
Alistair Darling looks after the money.
Letter from America had Alistair Cooke.
Cricket is played by Alistair Cook.
Alistair McGowan does impersonations.
Alistair Maclean writes literary creations.
Alistair Burt does politicking.
Alistair Campbell was good at spin.
Alistair's a great name and it's not fair
There'll never be a King Alistair.

24 hour news

And now we'll bring you news that's breaking.
We will tell you all that's happening.
This seems to be completely nothing.
And so to our man reporting
Who'll spend ages saying nothing
On what's happening, which is nothing.
Now we have Professor Bumbling,
Who's expert on completely nothing;
He'll spend ages saying nothing
On things that amount to nothing.
Sorry now we're interrupting;
There seem to be some things developing.
Our man on the spot is reporting
Right from where there's nothing happening.
(He could be anywhere – he is standing
By an anonymous-looking building).
What he has to say is nothing.
And so we will go now to Washing-
Ton, for the view on nothing
In the USA; it's nothing.
I hope I do things much more use
Than watch 24 hour news.

Khovanshchina

Musorgsky should have had more time to compose.
He had a full-time job, and drank far too much booze.
He never really finished this opera, that's so great,
Set back in the time of Peter the Great,
Who wanted Russia changed so it fits the modern day,
And woe betide anyone who stood in his way.
There's the bloodthirsty Streltsy, who are the private army
Of arrogant and proud Prince Ivan Khovansky.
Then there are the Old Believers; they're a problem 'cos
They want to keep the Russian faith just the way it was.
These are led by Dosifei (I s'pose he is chief vicar).
Dosifei's a priest with bagfuls of charisma.
The Old Believer Marfa with Andrei is besotted.
He's the son of Khovansky, and tells her to get knotted.
He doesn't care for her, and she will have to lump it.
He's chasing after Emma, a bit of German crumpet.
Golitsin is a big man; we see him in his room.
Marfa tells his fortune, and prophesies his doom.
Susanna, Old Believer, thinks Marfa has done wrong,
But all that Marfa's done is sing her little song.
Shaklovity is the Tsar's agent; he is really scary.
He brings about the downfall of Khovansky and the Streltsy.
He says that, against the Tsar, Khovansky has a plot,
And then he has Khovansky killed, and so that's his lot.

For Golitsin, Marfa's prophecy comes to fruition.
Forced into exile is now his position.
It seems that the Streltsy, to a man, will lose their heads,
But they are pardoned, and go home to their beds.
Surrounded by the troops, the Old Believers start a fire,
And burn themselves to death; this is their funeral pyre.
When this really happened d'you think they all said 'Hey!
We're going to be in an opera one day'?

Les Troyens

It's better than Carmen and it's better than Verdi.
Berlioz's opera is better than Puccini.
The Trojans are delighted when the Greeks disappear,
But Cassandra sees the future and she is filled with fear.
Nobody believes in what she has to say.
Not even Corebus, who is her fiancé.
Everybody thinks that the Greeks have gone for good,
Though they've left behind a horse made of wood.
Laocoön is suspicious, and it does seem funny.
He is eaten by two sea-monsters, and they both say 'Yummy!'.
So the hapless Trojans, into town, wheel the horse,
But inside it's filled up with soldiers, of course.
When they come out, they let the Greeks into the city.
They completely destroy it, which is such a pity.
The Trojan women kill themselves, and show a lot of bravery,
Rather than surrender, and submit themselves to slavery.
Aeneas and his men, with the treasure, get away.
They are bound for Italy, but they lose their way.
Their destiny in Italy is that they should found Rome,
For the gods have decreed this the new Trojan home.
Now Carthage is a city on the African shore.
Ruled by Queen Dido, it prospers more and more.
Though her husband's dead, she wants to stay a faithful wife.
Her sister Anna says to her: 'Come on, get a life'.
The Trojans arrive in this city of prosperity.
Queen Dido shows to them generous hospitality.

The first thing that the Trojans do is join the Carthaginians
In their war against Iarbas, king of the Numidians.
Dido likes Aeneas; she really, really likes 'im.
They go off on a hunt, and soon they are an item.
Narbal is worried that her queenly duties wait.
Anna says: 'Lighten up, can't you see it's great?'
But though the Trojans are among hospitable hosts,
'What about Italy?' say the Trojan ghosts.
Dido is so angry, she can scarcely believe
Aeneas and the Trojans will all pack up and leave.
(She's a queen, after all, and she's had the thought:
The way she has been treated is like any girl in port.)
When the fleet, with Aeneas and the Trojans, have all gone,
She stabs herself to death, when her funeral pyre she's on.
The Carthaginians blame Aeneas that they have a queen no more,
Carthage and the Romans would be foes for evermore.

Stupid Poem with Bob Dylan Songs

Her lottery ticket was lost, and nowhere to be found.
Perhaps, like a rolling stone, it was lying on the ground.
Perhaps, blowing in the wind, it had flown away.
So she asked her husband if he'd taken it away.
'It ain't me babe, I'm sure we had it safe last night.
Just like a woman! Don't think twice, it's alright.'
She had those subterranean homesick blues; she searched high and
low.
In Positively 4th Street and Desolation Row.
But times they are a-changin', the weather will get wet.
A hard rain's a-gonna fall, and she's not found it yet.
It was found by a percussionist in the Salvation Army band.
A chap called Mr. Tambourine Man had it in his hand.

The Big Bang

What's the most important thing that ever has occurred?
If I said 'My birthday', you would think this absurd.
Even more important: the Universe began
Some fourteen billion years ago in what's called the Big Bang.
We think that this was the Universe's start
From the way the galaxies are all moving apart.
If they are near, or if they're far away,
We know, from their spectra, that they're all moving away.
And everywhere we look, there's microwave radiation
That seems to be a remnant of the Universe's creation.
The amounts of the elements that we see today
Are just what you'd expect if it started this way.
What was there before? Some people have a hunch:
It all came together in what's called the Big Crunch.
Or it could be that this question has no meaning,
For only the Big Bang brought time into being.
If you want more, then you will be disappointed.
I cannot write more, for my brain has just exploded.

Orders of Classical Architecture

Next time that you build a temple,
Your choice of order won't be simple:
Corinthian, or it might be Doric.
We could make it, guv, Ionic.
Corinthian columns, would you believe,
Have on top a load of leaves.
Ionic columns have a scroll;
Doric ones have nowt at all.
The Parthenon, outside, is Doric.
Further in it is Ionic.
They thought it a real good wheeze
If all round they made a frieze.
They lost their marbles; you can see 'em,
Right now, in the British Museum.

Poème Stupide en Français (sort of)

Je parle French with fluency.
Fauré et Debussy.
Je sais lots of mots, see.
Frère Jacques et Sarkozy.
Je parle bien la langue.
Mange tout, vol au vent.
I have très bien taste.
Je n'aime pas fish paste.
Je préfère fish paté.
Je ne suis pas batty.
Je ne fais pas chips eat.
Donnez-moi pommes frîtes.
Cette poème est en Français
Parce qu'il est plus poncey.

Popular Songs

Why do birds suddenly appear
Every time you are near?
I guess you cannot see but
On your head there is a peanut.

My love is like a red, red rose.
She lives down in the sewer.
She is like a red rose 'cos
She grows well in manure.

I woke up, it was a Chelsea morning.
Odd, since I was in Dorking.

Rain Stops Play at the Battle of Hastings

We're the jolly Norman knights,
And we never shirk from fights.
We know the way when we're at all
Signposts when they point to 'Battle'.
We've crossed the Channel in a ship,
So William gets the kingship.
This place we will overrun,
When we get a bit of sun.
Conquering England ain't so brainy
As the place is always rainy.
Anyone would look a wally:
A suit of armour and a brolly.
They inspect the ground at four.
Then, with luck, we'll have some more
Fighting; there will be a battle:
One in the eye for King Harold.
Sunny weather is a fantasy
Shown in the Bayeaux Tapestry.

Historical Personages do their Laundry

Gengis Khan,
When he can,
Spends his Sundays
Washing undies.
Napoleon
Told Wellington:
'Sorry mate,
You'll have to wait.
I've got to get
To the launderette'.
Julius Caesar
Cleans his toga,
So he has
Non-biological Daz.
(Rubicon-crossing
Needs clean washing.)
He was a king,
But the tide came in,
So the dry cleaner
Was even keener
To clean the suit
Of King Canute.
Hannibal

Made sure all
His elephants
Had clean pants.
If we're candid,
Desert sand did
Not please Rameses,
On his dungerees.
In Nottingham Forest,
Robin Hood (honest)
Used to wear
Dirty underwear,
So Maid Marion
Said 'What a carry on!
Let them soak
You filthy bloke'.
Marie Antoinette
Got most upset
When a stain got
On her raincoat.
All the washing
Of Rasputin
Was made cleaner
By the tsarina.
The clothes King John
Chose to put on
For Magna Carta
Were much smarter.
In times medieval,
They didn't use Persil;

When things were feudal,
They used to do all
Washing historical
In Serf Biological.
Captain Cook
Would always look,
In his discoveries,
For washing facilities.
Shakespeare
Washed his gear:
You must have clean kit
Writing Hamlet.
Aristotle
Wondered what'll
He'd do: 'It's urgent,
I've no detergent'.
Robert the Bruce
Was smart and spruce.
George Washington
Put clean washing on.
The sweaters on
Jefferson
Got nice and clean
In the machine.
History's heroes
All wore clean clothes.

Cerberus

(in Greek mythology Cerberus was a monstrous
three-headed hound who guarded the entrance to
the Underworld)

The count of heads I have is more
Than two but less than four.
When I bark it's such a racket
The neighbours leave; they just can't hack it.
Also I can have a whale of a
Time licking my genitalia.
At food time to my bowls I come
I make short work of Pedigree Chum.
I manage to instil such fear
In any postman who comes near.
You'll get when you say 'Go fetch, boy',
A ball, a stick, a squeaky toy.
I carry them all at once, you see;
Three people can all play with me.
If you want to buy one lead,
Get a dog with just one head.

Mahler Symphonies

If you've ever heard Mahler's First Symphony,
You've heard Frère Jacques, but played in a minor key.
The Second Symphony's known as The Resurrection;
The choir and the orchestra are huge in every section.
The Third, with six movements, is also quite enormous.
The innocent, sunny Fourth has a more modest form as
The singer sings of Heaven as it's seen by a kiddie.
The Fifth starts funereal, but ends up rather jolly.
The Sixth is really tragic, from its start to its ending;
It's really not the music that you'd play at a wedding.
The Seventh was once used in a TV ad for oil.
The Symphony of a Thousand (number eight) is choral.
Gloomy and nostalgic is symphony number nine.
Finished by another, the Tenth sounds just fine.
Another symphonic work that's of Mahler's invention:
Das Lied von der Erde should also get a mention.

What the Celts said about the Anglo-Saxons

'British jobs for British workers.
Not these Anglo-Saxon shirkers.
Vortigern was such a berk.
That lot help us? It won't work.
First came Hengest and his brother Horsa.
This was followed by, of course, a
Load of Anglo-Saxon rabble.
In their English tongue they gabble.
They can't be arsed to lean our lingo.
It's really awful and, by jingo,
I hate to see our once-great nation
Threatened by mass immigration.
To let them in is just insanity,
And a threat to Christianity,
For they are a load of pagans;
Will they ever become Christians?
I will not stand for this; you see,
I'm off to join the BNP.'

(No-one lived in Britain once.
We all descend from immigrants.
Let this truth resound and ring:
Native British? No such thing.)

St. Francis of Assisi

St. Francis of Assisi
Came from Assisi,
So it's really easy
To remember where he's from, see.

Following this pattern,
If he came from Clapham,
He'd be Francis of Clapham.
But this did not happen.

If it were that France is
The birthplace of Francis,
Then Francis of France is
The full name of Francis.

Everyone in Assisi
Has the name 'of Assisi'.
There's Brenda of Assisi,
And Nigel of Assisi.

If everyone in Goring
Had the name 'of Goring',
The phone book in Goring
Would be very boring.

So if your aspiration
Is canonisation,
Put your home location
On your application.

Names That Don't Give a Clear Indication of Gender

If you say your child's called Roy,
I know straight off it is a boy,
But if you say your child's called Kim,
I can't tell if it's her or him.
If you tell me it's called Leslie,
It's just as likely she's called Lesley.
If you say the name is Francis,
Then the chance is she is Frances.
You cannot get more butch than Joe,
Unless, a girl, she is called Jo.
Ronnie is a gentleman's moniker,
But it also means Veronica.
These are names when said, you see,
You can't tell if it's he or she.
A group of people at the North Pole argue about the way to go

A Group of People at the North Pole Argue About the Way to Go

'We should continue going North,
Just like we did when we set forth.'
'I just don't think we have that option;
All ways are South, in each direction.'
'This is what I think is best:
We should start off going West.'
'Hear my point of view at least.
It would be best if we went East.'
'Don't you hear me when I say:
Going South's the only way?'
'Every path is South, you say?
How can we ever know the way?'
'While we're here we're getting old.
I tell you what: it's bloody cold!'

Highway Code – The Musical

I am sixteen going on seventeen,
Very soon I will be driving.
There may be trouble up ahead,
So the roadsigns must be read.
The hills are alive; I must change down.
I'll stick to thirty in the town.
Tie a yellow ribbon round
The old oak tree; this is sound,
But if a yellow line you spot,
Parking there, you must not.
Tonight won't be just any night;
I'll put on sidelights, to be seen alright.
I had a little drink about an hour ago;
I'll leave the car until tomorrow.
Not the crossbar, but the seat
Is the place that you'll look sweet
On a bicycle made for one;
The pavement you must not ride on.
The Highway Code would be more fun
If it were not read but sung.

Idomeneo

Most of Mozart's operas are really rather merrier,
You won't find any laughs, though, in this opera seria.
The Trojan princess Ilia is imprisoned on Crete.
It's really not so bad, though, in fact it is quite neat.
She loves Idamante, who is a real nice fellow.
He's the son of the king, who is called Idomeneo.
Since he loves her too, you would think that that is that,
But Elettra loves him also, and she's a fierce old bat.
Idomeneo is caught in a storm; he escapes from the waves.
He gives thanks to the gods, as his life they have saved.
And so in gratitude, the gods to appease,
He vows that he would sacrifice the first thing that he sees.
He really didn't think, when he made this vow so wild.
He first sees Idamante, who is his only child.
(You can say what you like about human sacrifice;
It makes for good opera, though it isn't nice).
He consults his adviser to find out what he'd say.
Arbace says 'Idamante must be got right out the way'.
And so that Idamante can be left in peace,
He'll accompany Elettra when she sails back to Greece.
The weather first is fine, but very soon gets worse.
Neptune is a god who is really rather cross.
Although he's been waiting, he's not had his sacrifice.
Now he sends a monster, the folk to terrorise.
Idamante is so brave though, and he slays the beast.

And now all the people can be left in peace.
Idamante will be sacrificed; he's ready to be dead,
But Ilia comes along and says: 'Kill me instead'.
Neptune now relents, and Idamante's king.
The people can rejoice, and happily they sing.

The Word for 'Milk' in Various Languages

The French are often heard to say:
'Donnez-moi a pint of lait'.
The Germans, when they have their brekky,
Ask for milch in their coffee.
(I don't suppose that it is much
Different when it's said in Dutch).
When Spanish milk 'ee goes to fetch, 'ee
Asks the shop for some leche.
The fridge she opens in her nighty,
In Portugal for some laite.
Moloko, of course, is white.
молоко's what the Russians write.
You can't expect that I would know at
All the word in Serbo-Croat.
In every country this is how
Milk is got: it's from a cow.

Why the Olympic Games Should be Held in Croydon

The Olympic Games have all been in
Moscow, Sydney and Beijing.
The next place that they will go
Is London; after that is Rio.
But one place that has been forgotten:
The city of the future: Croydon.
With transport links and hotel space,
It really is the ideal place.
It really would be just terrific
And just right for the games Olympic.
For track events and running races,
There are really lots of places.
There's Lloyd Park and Sandilands,
With lots of space for all the fans.
Of course you would need lots of heats.
These could take place in Thornton Heath.
It's fun to run a marathon
When it starts at Coulsdon.
The javelin would go down well
At the Selsdon Park Hotel.
Discus throwers? You could let 'em
Strut their funky stuff in Streatham.
Triple-jump would be very
Good if held at Norbury.
Water sports? Well, they could take

Place with ease on Norwood Lake.
And also a sports centre that is
Perfect is at Crystal Palace.
Swimming could be well worse,
If it's not in Selhust.
Boxing matches? They could all
Take their place in Fairfield Hall.
Weight-lifting? This would surely
Go down very well in Purley.
All the folk of Addington
Could go and watch the badminton.
Show-jumping? The riders said:
'Let's all go to Sanderstead'.
Fencing contests would be good
If they're held in Norwood.
Accommodation? You could stick 'em
In Addiscombe or West Wickham.
Croydon games would be superb.
(London is a minor suburb).

Iphigénie en Tauride

If you've ever got to know this opera by Gluck,
All I can say is that you have been in luck.
It's the finest work of a really good composer.
Why it's not known better is something of a poser.
Iphigenia's home background is not a happy one.
Her mum killed her dad, and her brother killed her mum.
Now she's far from home in Greece, in fact she is in Scythia.
Where she is high priestess at the temple of Diana.
With the king Thoas, she doesn't see eye-to-eye.
He says that she must sacrifice any foreign guy.
Thoas has strange ideas, and really is a thug you see.
(If he were around today, he'd be in the BNP).
The Scythians have just captured a pair of passing Greeks:
The sacrificial victims that cruel Thoas seeks.
She doesn't want to sacrifice either of these guys.
It's really not her thing – in fact she's rather nice.
What she doesn't realise is that one of them's Orestes,
Who is her long-lost brother; the other is Pylades.
She thinks that she can save one of them at least;
He can take a letter to her folks back in Greece.
It's not an easy choice, but she fixes on Orestes,
But he says: 'I'll kill myself, you must save Pylades'.
'Orestes is dead', Orestes tells her falsely.
She sings a lament, which is really rather lovely.
Gradually she realises who he really is.
He's her long-lost brother, and she's his long-lost sis.
Pylades comes with help he's brought back from Greece, and so as,
In the nick of time, he can overthrow Thoas.
Diana, who is goddess, says: 'Let us end the folly
Of Thoas and his crew', and it all ends rather jolly.

Lightning Source UK Ltd.
Milton Keynes UK
14 January 2010

148544UK00003B/3/P